WW kitchen collection

Veggie

Mushroom & chestnut pie, page 106

Baked sweet potatoes with veggie chilli, page 60

Turmeric broth bowl with beans, veg & noodles, page 108

Pea, mint & créme fraîche soup, page 14

Veggie

The small print

EGGS We use medium eggs, unless otherwise stated. Pregnant women, the elderly and children should avoid recipes with eggs which are raw or not fully cooked.

FRUIT AND VEGETABLES Recipes use medium-size fruit and veg, unless otherwise stated.

LIGHT SOFT CHEESE Where a recipe uses reduced-fat soft cheese, we mean a soft cheese with 30% less fat than its full-fat equivalent.

LOW-FAT SPREAD When a recipe uses a low-fat spread, we mean a spread with a fat content of no more than 39%.

MICROWAVES If we have used a microwave in any of our recipes, the timings will be for an 850-watt microwave oven.

PREP AND COOK TIMES These are approximate and meant to be guidelines only. The prep time includes all the steps up to and following the main cooking time(s). The stated cook times may vary according to your oven.

VEGETARIAN ITALIAN HARD CHEESE Where we reference this in vegetarian recipes, we mean a cheese similar to parmesan (which is not vegetarian) but which is suitable for vegetarians.

GLUTEN FREE Recipes displaying the gluten free icon include ingredients that naturally do not contain gluten, but may also contain processed products, such as sauces, stock cubes and spice mixes. If so, you should ensure that those products do not include any gluten-containing ingredients (wheat, barley or rye) – these will be highlighted in the ingredients list on the product's label. Manufacturers may also indicate whether there is a chance that their product may have been accidentally contaminated with gluten during the manufacturing process. For more information and guidance on gluten-free products, visit www.coeliac.org.uk

SMARTPOINTS have been calculated using the values for generic foods, not brands (except where stated). Tracking using branded items may affect the recorded SmartPoints.

Seven C3

Produced by Seven Publishing on behalf of Weight Watchers International, Inc. Published August 2017. All rights reserved. No part of this publication may be reproduced, stored in a retrieval system or transmitted in any form by any means, electronic, mechanical photocopying, recording or otherwise, without the prior written permission of Seven Publishing.

First published in Great Britain by Seven Publishing Ltd. Copyright © 2017, Weight Watchers International, Inc.

Seven Publishing Ltd
3-7 Herbal Hill
London
EC1R 5EJ
www.seven.co.uk

This book is copyright under the Berne Convention. No reproduction without permission. All rights reserved.

10 9 8 7 6 5 4 3 2 1

Weight Watchers SmartPoints and the SmartPoints icon are the registered trademarks of Weight Watchers International, Inc and are used under license by Weight Watchers (UK) Ltd. All rights reserved.

A CIP catalogue record for this book is available from the British Library. ISBN: 978-0-9935835-7-5

WEIGHT WATCHERS PUBLICATIONS TEAM Samantha Rees, Nicola Kirk, Stephanie Williams, Ruby Bamford, Nicola Hill

PHOTOGRAPHY Kris Kirkham

RECIPES & FOOD STYLING Sarah Cook
ADDITIONAL RECIPES & STYLING
Bianca Nice, Polly Webb-Wilson, Hannah Yeadon

PROP STYLING Sarah Birks
ADDITIONAL STYLING Linda Berlin, Lydia Brun, Luis Peral

FOR SEVEN PUBLISHING LTD

EDITORIAL & DESIGN
Editor-in-Chief Helen Renshaw
Editor Ward Hellewell Sub editors Chloe Hay, Sarah Peak
Art director Liz Baird
Picture editor Carl Palmer

FOOD TEAM
Food editor Sarah Akhurst
Senior food assistant Nadine Brown
Food assistant Gabriella English
Nutritionist Alexandra Harris

ACCOUNT MANAGEMENT
Account manager Gina Cavaciuti
Business director, retail Andy Roughton
Group publishing director Kirsten Price

PRODUCTION
Production director Sophie Dillon
Colour reproduction by F1 Colour Printed in the UK by CPI Colour

Contents

More and more of us are choosing to include meat-free meals in our diet, whether it's once-a-week or more often. Why? Well, going *veggie* has lots of *benefits*.

As well as being cheaper and kinder to the environment, eating less meat and *more vegetables* is healthier, too. In this book, the Weight Watchers Kitchen Team has come up with a collection of *delicious, easy* recipes that take advantage of the incredible variety of vegetables, grains, pulses and other meat-free ingredients out there.

From quick and *easy dishes* that are great for brunch or lunch, to more hearty meals for dinnertime, we've pulled out all the stops to ensure that every recipe is not only achievable, but is nutritious and *great-tasting* too. They've all been tried and tested, and the SmartPoints are worked out for each recipe, making it easy for you to be inspired and stay on track.

So if you want to try eating less meat or perhaps even go all the way and become fully vegetarian, you'll find there are plenty of *ideas* inside to get you started.

LOOK OUT FOR THE SYMBOLS BELOW:

 The number inside the SmartPoints coin tells you how many SmartPoints are in the serving.

If you're following No Count, you can eat this recipe to your satisfaction without having to count it. You can also have 2 teaspoons of healthy oil per day (olive, sunflower, safflower, rapeseed or flaxseed).

GF A recipe that is totally gluten free, or can be made gluten free with a few simple swaps (see page 6).

V Indicates a recipe that is vegetarian

* Indicates a recipe that is suitable for freezing (without garnishes or side dishes).

for meat-free cooking

If you're choosing to go meat-free, whether it's all the time or once in a while, here are a few easy ways to get maximum flavour with minimum effort…

Make a change

Don't just stick with the trusty old standby veg you know and love – try something new. Never had celeriac or pak choi? Now's the time to give them a go!

Pack in the flavour

For really intense flavour, try slow-roasting your veg. Squash, carrots, sweet potatoes, peppers, onions, tomatoes and cauliflower are all especially great slow-roasted. Make a big batch and use them in all sorts of dishes throughout the week.

Don't overcook

Melt-in-the-mouth veg is perfect in a slow-cooked casserole, but most vegetables will benefit from less cooking, rather than more. Keep dishes like stir-fries tasting fresh by lightly cooking the veg so it retains its crunch.

Stock up on spices

Spices and herbs are great for giving veg an instant flavour hit. A jar of mixed herbs and a pepper grinder are the absolute minimum you need to create delicious veggie food. Add to this cumin, paprika, chilli flakes, oregano, rosemary and thyme, and the possible flavour combinations you can create will be endless.

Buy seasonal

When veg is in season it not only tastes its absolute best, but it will be at its cheapest too.

Eat the rainbow

We eat with our eyes, as well as our mouths, so when food looks good, it's that much more appetising. Fortunately, veg comes in an amazing range of colours, so it's not hard to make your meals look good, and if you include a variety of different hues in your meal, you'll be packing in a wide range of nutrients too.

Best for your budget

Cooking veggie food doesn't have to be expensive. It really pays to shop around so you can get the best deal on veg – your local greengrocer may be cheaper than the supermarket. To keep your storecupboard full and save money, look out for big bags of dried lentils or beans, and grains like bulgur wheat and brown rice.

Go for tins

Tinned veg has its uses. Keep a supply of chopped tomatoes, sweetcorn, carrots, artichokes, peas and potatoes in your storecupboard, as well as tinned fruit, beans and legumes. When fresh supplies are running low, you'll always be able to whip up a delicious meat-free meal.

Keep a balance

Just because you're skipping the meat doesn't mean you should overdo it on the carbs. Stay aware of portion control when it comes to rice, pasta and potatoes.

Fill your freezer

A good supply of frozen veg, Quorn and soya products will help you stay on track when you're in need of a speedy meal. Frozen veg can be just as nutritious as the fresh stuff and there's so many different varieties to choose from. Frozen herbs and spices make great instant flavour boosters too.

Missing meat?

Make meat-free meals feel satisfying and substantial by using ingredients that add a variety of different textures and flavours. Here are some veggie favourites to get you started:

Tofu

On its own, tofu is bland, but its sponge-like texture means it soaks up loads of flavour from marinades and sauces, which makes it great for stir-fries and curries. Made from soya beans, it comes in different varieties and degrees of firmness – 'silken' tofu is soft and delicate, while regular tofu is firmer and chewier. Try our tofu kebabs & rice salad (p62); and Cajun-style tofu with corn salsa & crispy salad (p76).

Quorn

A meat substitute made from a high-protein fungus, Quorn has a meaty texture and comes in lots of varieties, including mince, pieces, fillets and sausages. Like tofu, it will absorb flavours from other ingredients. You can use it pretty much as you would meat, so the mince makes a great lasagne, and the pieces are great in stir-fries. Try our Quorn keema curry (p70); and Quorn fajitas with cheese & soured cream (p52).

Mushrooms

With their rich, earthy flavour and meaty texture, mushrooms make a great stand-in for meat in so many dishes, including soups, casseroles and curries. A whole grilled portobello mushroom makes a super-quick veggie burger, while oyster mushrooms, with their more delicate flavour, are great in stir-fries. Try our roasted mushroom pasta (p64), or chipotle mushroom nachos (p16).

Aubergines

Another veg with a meaty texture, by itself aubergine has a very subtle flavour but it absorbs other flavours beautifully so it's great for marinating. There are lots of ways to enjoy it – cut it into 'steaks' then marinate and cook on a griddle, or roast it then whizz into a tasty dip. Try our aubergine pizza slices with mozzarella & basil (p18); and soy-roasted aubergines with fragrant rice (p54).

Pulses & beans

Lentils, chickpeas and beans – there are lots of different varieties and they make almost any dish much more substantial. They're inexpensive too, so perfect if you're on a budget. Dried ones are especially cheap, but keep tinned ones in your storecupboard as well, for when you're in a hurry. Great in soups, stews, curries and salads. Try our mushroom & lentil ragù with boodles (p46).

Eggs

With a few fresh eggs to hand, you'll never be stuck for a quick, easy and satisfying meat-free meal. A source of protein, they're simple to cook and incredibly versatile – enjoy them poached, fried, soft- or hard-boiled, in a salad or whisked into a creamy quiche – there's all sorts of delicious ways to use them. Try our roasted vegetable quiche (p92); and potato nests with baked eggs & kale (p26).

Pea, mint & crème fraîche soup

Serves 4

Prep time
10 minutes

Cook time
13 minutes

Using frozen peas means this colourful soup couldn't be easier, and it's full of beautiful, fresh flavours too.

Ingredients
Calorie controlled cooking spray
4 spring onions, trimmed and chopped
1 garlic clove, minced
650g petits pois, defrosted
650ml vegetable stock, made with 1 stock cube
100g young leaf spinach
Handful fresh mint leaves, plus extra to garnish
100g half-fat crème fraîche, plus 4 teaspoons to serve
Grated zest of 1 lemon and juice of ½

1 Mist a large, deep pan with cooking spray and put over a medium heat. Add the spring onions and garlic, then cook for 2-3 minutes until starting to soften.

2 Add the peas and stock, then simmer for 10 minutes until the peas are tender. Remove from the heat and reserve a scoop of the peas for the garnish.

3 Add the spinach, mint, 100g crème fraîche, half the lemon zest and all of the lemon juice to the pan. Blend with a hand-held blender until smooth, then season well. Mix the remaining crème fraîche with 3 teaspoons of water. Serve the soup drizzled with the thinned crème fraîche and garnished with the reserved peas, mint leaves and the remaining lemon zest.

SmartPoints
3 per serving

See page 6

Chipotle mushroom nachos

Serves 4

Prep time
15 minutes

Cook time
20 minutes

Who doesn't love nachos? This healthier version has all the flavour, but fewer SmartPoints.

Ingredients
4 wholemeal wraps
Calorie controlled cooking spray
1 onion, thinly sliced
1 red pepper, deseeded and cut into 2cm pieces
275g flat Portobello mushrooms, thickly sliced
400g tin chopped tomatoes
2 teaspoons chipotle paste
40g 0% fat natural Greek yogurt
50g reduced-fat Cheddar cheese, grated
Handful fresh coriander, roughly chopped

1 Preheat the oven to 200°C, fan 180°C, gas mark 6. Cut the wraps into tortilla chip-sized triangles and spread out on 2 baking sheets. Mist with cooking spray and season well. Bake in the oven for 7-8 minutes or until crisp and browned at the edges, then set aside.

2 Meanwhile, mist a large pan with cooking spray, add the onion and cook over a medium heat for 6-8 minutes, stirring, until soft and just starting to colour. Add the pepper and mushrooms, and cook for a further 5 minutes, until they start to soften.

3 Strain the tomatoes and set aside the juice. In a small jug, stir the tomatoes, chipotle paste and yogurt together, then pour over the veg mixture and simmer for 5 minutes, uncovered, until the sauce is slightly reduced. If it gets too dry, add a splash of the reserved tomato juice. Season well.

4 Preheat the grill to medium. Put the tortilla chips in an ovenproof serving dish and top with the mushroom chilli. Sprinkle over the grated cheese, then put under the grill until melted and bubbling. Sprinkle over the chopped coriander to serve.

SmartPoints
6 per serving

Aubergine pizza slices with mozzarella & basil

Serves 4

Prep time
10 minutes

Cook time
20 minutes

Using slices of aubergine as the base of these mini pizzas makes them very low in SmartPoints.

Ingredients
3 aubergines
Calorie controlled cooking spray
1 small onion, finely chopped
1 garlic clove, crushed
1 teaspoon dried oregano
400g tin chopped tomatoes
125g reduced-fat mozzarella, roughly torn
Small handful fresh basil leaves

1 Preheat the oven to 200°C, fan 180°C, gas mark 6. Put a wire rack on a baking sheet. Slice each aubergine into 8 rounds, about 1.5cm thick. Arrange the aubergine rounds on the wire rack and mist with cooking spray. Bake for 12-15 minutes until golden, turning over and misting with cooking spray again halfway through the cooking time.

2 Meanwhile make the sauce. Mist a pan with cooking spray and cook the onion for 3-4 minutes, until it starts to soften. Add the garlic and cook for another minute. Stir in the oregano and chopped tomatoes, season, then simmer for 10 minutes until slightly reduced.

3 Preheat the grill. When the aubergines are cooked, remove them from the oven and spread each one with the tomato sauce. Scatter over the mozzarella and top with the basil, reserving some of the leaves to garnish. Place under the grill for 2-3 minutes until the mozzarella is melted and golden. Garnish with the reserved basil leaves, then serve.

SmartPoints
2 per 6 rounds

See page 6

Tip
You can save time by making the sauce in advance – it will keep in the fridge for up to 4 days.

Root veg chips with spicy yogurt dip

Serves 4

Prep time
15 minutes

Cook time
55 minutes

This twist on traditional chips get a flavour makeover with a spicy yogurt dip. Great as a side dish or snack.

Ingredients
2 beetroot
1 large potato
450g butternut squash
2 teaspoons sunflower oil
150g 0% fat natural
Greek yogurt
2 teaspoons ras el hanout

1 Preheat the oven to 220°C, fan 200°C, gas mark 7. Scrub and peel the beetroot and cut into 1.5cm-thick chips. Put the chips in a roasting tin. Peel and slice the potato and squash into 1.5cm-thick chips and put them in another roasting tin.

2 Drizzle the oil over the vegetables, season well, and toss with your hands to coat, then arrange in a single layer in the tins. Bake for 50-55 minutes, turning every 20 minutes, until the chips are cooked through and golden brown.

3 Meanwhile, in a small bowl, combine the yogurt with the ras el hanout and season well. Serve with the chips.

SmartPoints
2 per serving

See page 6

Cauliflower tabbouleh with griddled halloumi

Serves 4

Prep time
15 minutes
+ cooling

Cook time
8 minutes

This wheat-free version of the classic Middle Eastern salad is topped with delicious halloumi cheese.

Ingredients
1 large cauliflower
Calorie controlled cooking spray
300g cherry tomatoes, halved
1 cucumber, diced
20 green olives
Handful fresh parsley, roughly chopped
Handful fresh mint, roughly chopped
Juice of 1 lemon
250g pack reduced-fat halloumi cheese

1 Roughly chop the cauliflower and put in a food processor. Blitz until it resembles couscous.

2 Mist a large frying pan with cooking spray and set over a medium heat. Fry the cauliflower for 3-4 minutes, until it has started to soften. Set aside to cool.

3 When the cauliflower is cool, add the tomatoes, cucumber, olives, parsley, mint and lemon juice, then stir to combine. Season well.

4 Cut the halloumi into 12 slices. Mist a frying pan or griddle with cooking spray and fry the cheese for 2 minutes on each side, until golden. Serve 3 halloumi slices on top of the cauliflower tabbouleh per serving.

SmartPoints
6 per serving

See page 6

Serves 4

Prep time
10 minutes

Cook time
45 minutes

Roasted carrot salad with rocket & goat's cheese

A simple, colourful salad served with mild, creamy goat's cheese that's flavoured with fresh dill.

Ingredients
750g carrots, small ones left whole, large ones cut into thick slices
1 tablespoon olive oil
100g sourdough bread, cut in 2mm slices
Calorie controlled cooking spray
2 x 150g tubs of Chavroux pure goat's cheese
2 tablespoons finely chopped fresh dill
80g rocket
Lemon wedges, to serve

1 Preheat the oven to 200°C, fan 180°C, gas mark 6. Put the carrots in a roasting tin and drizzle with the oil. Season and roast in the oven for 40 minutes, or until soft. Remove from the oven and set aside to cool to room temperature.

2 Meanwhile, put the sourdough bread slices on a baking sheet and mist with cooking spray. Bake in the oven for 5-6 minutes, or until crisp and golden. Remove from the oven and set aside.

3 Meanwhile, in a small bowl, mix the goat's cheese with the dill.

4 To serve, toss the carrots through the rocket and divide between plates. Add a large spoonful of the goat's cheese mixture to each and serve with the sourdough toasts and lemon wedges.

SmartPoints
8 per serving

Tip
You can bulk up this dish with plenty of extra salad, if you like.

Potato nests with baked eggs & kale

Makes 6

Prep time
20 minutes

Cook time
40-47 minutes

Having these for breakfast? Prepare the nests the night before to make it super speedy.

Ingredients
**Calorie controlled
cooking spray
400g floury potatoes,
coarsely grated
6 eggs, plus 1 yolk
100g kale**

1 Preheat the oven to 200°C, fan 180°C, gas mark 6. Mist 6 large non-stick muffin-tray holes with cooking spray. Put the grated potato on a clean tea towel and squeeze out the excess liquid. Put in a small bowl and mix with the egg yolk. Season to taste.

2 Divide the potato mixture between the 6 muffin holes, spreading it up the sides. Mist with cooking spray and bake for 30-35 minutes, or until golden brown and just cooked through. Remove from the oven and reduce the oven temperature to 180°C, fan 160°C, gas mark 4.

3 Meanwhile, bring a pan of water to a boil, add the kale and cook for 4-5 minutes, or until just tender, then drain and pat dry on kitchen paper.

4 Divide the kale between the 6 potato nests and crack an egg into each one. Bake for 10-12 minutes, until the egg is just set, then serve.

SmartPoints
2 per nest

See page 6

Smashed chickpeas with courgettes & feta

Serves 4

Prep time
20 minutes

Cook time
15 minutes

The combination of lemon and cumin with the saltiness of the feta in this dish is a taste explosion.

Ingredients

Calorie controlled
cooking spray
1 small onion, finely chopped
2 garlic cloves, minced
2 x 400g tins chickpeas,
drained and rinsed
3 tablespoons half-fat
crème fraîche
1 teaspoon cumin seeds
2 courgettes
Zest of 1 lemon, plus
2 tablespoons juice
75g tahini paste
2 tablespoons
pomegranate juice
50g light feta cheese,
crumbled
3 tablespoons
pomegranate seeds

1 Mist a saucepan with cooking spray, add the onion and cook over a medium heat for 8-10 minutes until soft and slightly golden. Add the garlic and cook for a further 3 minutes, then add the chickpeas and cook for 1 minute more. Take the pan off the heat, then add the crème fraîche and 3 tablespoons warm water. Use a potato masher to crush the chickpeas to a rough purée. Season, then cover and set aside to keep warm.

2 Put a small frying pan over a medium-high heat and add the cumin seeds. Toast for 1-2 minutes until fragrant, then transfer to a pestle and mortar and grind coarsely. Peel the courgettes into long ribbons and toss with the cumin and lemon zest, then set aside.

3 For the dressing, in a small jug, whisk together the lemon juice, tahini, pomegranate juice and 75ml warm water until smooth. Spoon the smashed chickpeas onto serving plates and top with the courgettes. Scatter over the feta and pomegranate seeds, then serve with the tahini sauce.

SmartPoints
7 per serving

Sweet potato & black bean quesadillas

Serves 4

Prep time
10 minutes

Cook time
45 minutes +
cooling

Tortilla wraps are filled with a delicious mix of beans, sweet potato and cheese, then grilled in a pan.

Ingredients

300g sweet potato, diced
½ tablespoon olive oil
400g tin black beans, drained and rinsed
250g vine tomatoes, roughly chopped
Zest and juice of 1 lime, plus extra wedges to serve
Handful of fresh coriander, leaves picked and roughly chopped
75g Weight Watchers Reduced Fat Grated Mature Cheese
4 Weight Watchers White Wraps
100g 0% fat natural Greek yogurt
Salad leaves, to serve

1 Preheat the oven to 200°C, fan 180°C, gas mark 6. Put the sweet potato in a roasting tin and drizzle with the oil. Season and roast for 30 minutes until tender. Transfer to a bowl and set aside to cool.

2 Mix the beans, tomatoes, lime juice, coriander and cheese into the cooled sweet potato.

3 Put 1 wrap in a non-stick frying pan and top with half of the bean mixture, leaving a narrow border around the edge. Put another wrap on top, then press down gently. Cook over a medium heat, pressing on the quesadilla, for 3-4 minutes or until the underside is golden. Carefully flip the quesadilla with a spatula and cook until the underside is toasted and the cheese is melted. Remove from the pan and repeat with the rest of the filling and tortillas. Cut into quarters.

4 Combine the yogurt and lime zest in a bowl. Serve 2 quesadilla quarters per person with the salad, yogurt and lime wedges.

SmartPoints
8 per serving

Spiced corn fritters with spinach & poached eggs

Harissa is a North African chilli paste – using it in these moreish fritters gives them a spicy kick.

Serves 4

Prep time
10 minutes

Cook time
15 minutes

Ingredients
100g plain flour
1 teaspoon baking powder
1 egg, lightly beaten
100ml skimmed milk
325g tin sweetcorn, drained
1 tablespoon harissa paste
2 spring onions,
finely chopped
1 tablespoon
fresh coriander, chopped
Calorie controlled
cooking spray
4 eggs
200g young leaf spinach
4 tablespoons 0% fat
natural Greek yogurt
Pinch smoked paprika

1 Sift together the plain flour and baking powder into a large bowl. Stir in the egg, milk, sweetcorn, harissa paste, spring onions and coriander, and stir until well combined.

2 Mist a non-stick frying pan with cooking spray. Put spoonfuls of the mixture into the pan to make 12 fritters. You'll need to do this in batches, cooking the fritters for 1-2 minutes on each side until golden brown.

3 Meanwhile, poach the eggs in a pan of simmering water. Put the spinach in a covered dish and microwave on high for 2 minutes to wilt, then divide it between 4 serving plates.

4 Serve the fritters on the spinach, topped with a poached egg and drizzle with the yogurt. Sprinkle with a little smoked paprika to garnish.

SmartPoints
3 per serving

Serves 4

Prep time
10 minutes

Cook time
20 minutes

Roasted broccoli & soba noodle salad

This colourful Asian-style salad is so much healthier than a takeaway, but tastes just as good.

Ingredients
1 head of broccoli,
broken into florets (larger
ones halved)
Calorie controlled
cooking spray
200g soba noodles
Juice of 2 limes
2 tablespoons soy sauce
1 tablespoon sesame oil
1 red chilli, deseeded and
finely chopped
Small handful of fresh
coriander, roughly chopped
3 spring onions, sliced

1 Preheat the oven to 200°C, fan 180°C, gas mark 6. Spread the broccoli out on a baking sheet and mist with cooking spray. Roast for 20 minutes, turning halfway through, until golden and just softened, then set aside to cool.

2 Meanwhile, cook the soba noodles to pack instructions until just cooked, then drain and run under cold water.

3 Mix together the lime juice, soy sauce, sesame oil and chilli. Put the noodles and broccoli in a bowl and toss with the dressing, coriander and spring onions, then serve.

SmartPoints
7 per serving

34

Loaded sweet potato tacos

Serves 4

Prep time
15 minutes + cooling
Cook time
25 minutes

Smoked paprika adds lots of spicy flavour
to the filling of these delicious veggie tacos.

Ingredients

350g sweet potato, diced
Calorie controlled
cooking spray
½ teaspoon smoked paprika
400g tin black beans,
drained and rinsed
1 red onion, finely diced
2 tomatoes, finely diced
2 tablespoons fresh
coriander, chopped
Juice of 1 lime
8 taco shells
(we used Old El Paso)
100g mixed salad leaves

1 Preheat the oven to 220°C, fan 200°C, gas mark 7. Put the sweet potato on a large baking sheet, mist with cooking spray and toss with the paprika until evenly coated. Roast for 20 minutes, until tender and just starting to brown. Transfer to a large bowl and set aside to cool completely.

2 Add the black beans, onion, tomatoes, coriander and lime juice to the cooled sweet potatoes. Season to taste and toss to combine.

3 To serve, heat the taco shells to pack instructions, fill with the salad leaves and top with the sweet potato mixture.

SmartPoints
7 per serving

See page 6

Tip
You could serve this
with 25g reduced-fat
soured cream
per person, for an
extra 2 SmartPoints
per serving.

Cauliflower toasts with spicy baked beans

A whole new way to serve beans on toast – after trying this, you'll never want to go back!

Serves 4

Prep time
25 minutes

Cook time
30 minutes

Ingredients

1 large cauliflower, trimmed and cut into florets
100g Weight Watchers Reduced Fat Grated Mature Cheese
2 eggs, beaten
1 teaspoon garlic granules
1 teaspoon dried oregano
½ teaspoon ground nutmeg
Calorie controlled cooking spray
1 small onion, finely chopped
2 garlic cloves, minced
1½ teaspoons hot paprika
½ teaspoon cumin seeds
¼ teaspoon ground cinnamon
Large pinch of ground cloves
1 tablespoon tomato purée
400g tin chopped tomatoes
2 bay leaves
2 x 400g tins cannellini beans, rinsed and drained
Small handful of flat-leaf parsley, roughly chopped

1 Pre-heat the oven to 200°C, fan 180°C, gas mark 6. Blitz the cauliflower in a food processor until it's the texture of rice. Put in a microwave-proof bowl and cover with clingfilm. Microwave on high for 4 minutes, stirring halfway through.

2 Leave to cool for 1 minute, then tip onto a clean tea towel. Squeeze all the excess moisture out of the cauliflower until dry. Tip it back into the bowl and mix in the cheese, eggs, garlic granules, dried oregano and nutmeg. Season well.

3 Line a baking tray with greaseproof paper and shape the cauliflower into 8 'toasts' on the tray. Bake for 20 minutes until crisp and golden at the edges.

4 Meanwhile, mist a large pan with cooking spray. Add the onion and cook for 6-8 minutes until softened and just starting to colour. Add the garlic and cook for a further 30 seconds, then stir in all the spices and tomato purée and cook for an additional 1 minute, stirring continuously.

5 Add the chopped tomatoes. Half fill the tin with water and add this to the pot, along with the bay leaves. Simmer, uncovered, for 10 minutes. Stir in the beans and cook with the lid on for a further 10 minutes until the beans are heated through and tender. Season well.

6 Serve the baked beans with the cauliflower toasts and a sprinkling of parsley.

SmartPoints
2 per serving

See page 6

Asparagus & lemon pearl barley risotto

This simple risotto uses barley instead of rice, and showcases the lovely fresh flavour of the asparagus.

Serves 4

Prep time
15 minutes

Cook time
40 minutes

Ingredients
250g asparagus, trimmed
Calorie controlled cooking spray
1 onion, finely chopped
2 celery sticks, finely chopped
½ teaspoon fennel seeds
1 garlic clove, crushed
225g pearl barley
1.25 litres hot vegetable stock, made with 2 stock cubes
Zest and juice of 1 lemon
Handful of fresh mint leaves, finely chopped, plus extra leaves to garnish

1 Slice the asparagus diagonally, keeping the tips in one piece. Set aside.

2 Heat a large sauté pan misted with cooking spray. Add the onion, celery and fennel seeds, then cook, stirring, for 4-5 minutes until the vegetables are soft. Add the garlic and cook for a minute more.

3 Stir in the barley. Cook, stirring, for 2 minutes, then gradually pour in 1 litre of the stock, stirring after each addition, making sure all liquid is absorbed before adding more. This will take about 20 minutes on a low heat.

4 Add the asparagus with the final 250ml of stock and cook for 10-12 minutes, or until the barley is tender.

5 Remove the pan from the heat, stir in the juice and most of the lemon zest, along with the chopped mint. Season to taste and serve scattered with the mint leaves and remaining zest.

SmartPoints
7 per serving

Butternut squash falafels

These 'falafels with a twist' have roasted butternut squash added, which gives them loads of flavour.

Serves 4

Prep time
30 minutes + chilling
Cook time
40 minutes

Ingredients
300g butternut squash
2 garlic cloves, unpeeled
Calorie controlled cooking spray
1 teaspoon each cumin and coriander seeds
1 red onion, finely chopped
400g tin chickpeas, drained
45g wholemeal breadcrumbs
Handful fresh flat-leaf parsley, chopped

For the sauce
Handful each fresh coriander and flat-leaf parsley, chopped
2 green finger chillies
3 garlic cloves
½ teaspoon each ground coriander and ground cumin
½ tablespoon white vinegar
Juice of 1 lemon
180g 0% fat natural Greek yogurt

For the salad
2 tablespoons pomegranate molasses
Juice of 1 lemon
3 large carrots, grated
1 red onion, finely sliced
Handful fresh mint, chopped

1 Preheat the oven to 200°C, fan 180°C, gas mark 6. Make the falafels. Peel and cut the squash into cubes, then put it in a roasting tin, along with the garlic. Mist with cooking spray and season. Roast for 30 minutes, then set aside to cool.

2 Meanwhile, dry-fry the cumin and coriander seeds in a small frying pan for 2 minutes until they start to pop. Transfer to a spice blender or pestle and mortar, then crush to a fine powder.

3 Mist the frying pan with cooking spray and fry the onion over a medium heat for 5 minutes.

4 Put the roasted squash and the chickpeas into a food processor and blitz to combine. Transfer to a bowl, add the spice mixture, cooked onion, breadcrumbs and parsley, and combine. Shape into 12 patties and chill in the fridge for 2 hours.

5 Meanwhile, make the sauce. Blitz all the ingredients in a food processor with a pinch of salt.

6 Mist a large non-stick frying pan with cooking spray and cook the falafels for 5 minutes on each side, until cooked through and golden.

7 Make the salad: in a bowl, whisk together the molasses and lemon juice, then season well. Put the carrot, red onion and mint in a bowl, drizzle over the dressing and toss to combine.

8 To serve, divide the salad between plates, top with the falafels and spoon over the sauce. You can freeze the falafels without the salad and yogurt.

SmartPoints
2 per serving

Mushroom & lentil ragù with boodles

Serves 4

Prep time
20 minutes

Cook time
45 minutes

If you love spaghetti Bolognese, try this all-veggie version served with spiralised butternut squash.

Ingredients

Calorie controlled
cooking spray
1 onion, finely chopped
1 large carrot, finely diced
1 celery stick, finely diced
3 cloves garlic, crushed
1 tablespoon fresh rosemary,
finely chopped
250g pack chestnut
mushrooms, sliced
200g dried Puy
lentils, rinsed
400g tin chopped tomatoes
400ml vegetable stock,
made with 1 stock cube
1 tablespoon tomato purée
2 bay leaves
2 teaspoons dried oregano
600g spiralised
butternut squash

1 Mist a large pan with cooking spray and put over a medium heat. Add the onion, carrot and celery, then cook for 10 minutes or until soft and lightly golden.

2 Stir in the garlic and rosemary and cook for a further minute, then add the mushrooms and cook for 3 minutes, until softened.

3 Add the Puy lentils, tomatoes, stock, tomato purée, bay leaves and oregano, then season to taste. Bring to a simmer and cook with the lid on for 30 minutes, until the lentils are tender and the sauce has thickened.

4 Meanwhile, put the butternut squash noodles in a microwave-proof bowl, cover and cook on high for 3 minutes, stirring halfway through the cooking time. Divide them between 4 plates and top with the ragù. You can freeze the ragù without the boodles.

0 SmartPoints value

SmartPoints
0 per serving

See page 6

Tip
You can also cook the boodles on a baking tray in the oven at 200°C, fan 180°C, gas mark 6, for 8 minutes. Mist with cooking spray first.

Warm squash, red onion & chickpea salad

Baharat is an aromatic Middle Eastern spice blend that you can find in most supermarkets.

Serves 4

Prep time
20 minutes

Cook time
35 minutes

Ingredients

1 small butternut squash, halved lengthways, deseeded and cut into wedges
Calorie controlled cooking spray
1 tablespoon baharat
200g baby spinach
1 red onion, thinly sliced
400g tin chickpeas, drained and rinsed
Small bunch fresh coriander, leaves picked and roughly chopped, plus a few extra sprigs to garnish

For the dressing

1 teaspoon smoked paprika
½ teaspoon ground cumin
Juice of 1 orange
2 teaspoons olive oil

1 Preheat the oven to 200°C, fan 180°C, gas mark 6. Mist the squash with the cooking spray, then toss with the baharat so it's evenly coated.

2 Spread the squash out evenly on a baking tray and roast for 20 minutes. Turn the wedges over, then roast for another 15 minutes, or until the butternut squash is tender. Remove from the oven.

3 Meanwhile, for the dressing, put all the ingredients in a small, clean jar, then season with salt and freshly ground black pepper. Put the lid on and shake the jar until combined. Chill until needed.

4 When ready to serve, put the spinach, onion, chickpeas and coriander in a bowl. Toss with the dressing. Top with the roasted squash and garnish with the extra coriander.

SmartPoints
1 per serving

See page 6

Red Thai coconut curry

This veggie version of the ever-popular Thai curry uses broccoli and aubergine.

Serves 4

Prep time
20 minutes

Cook time
20 minutes

Ingredients

Calorie controlled
cooking spray
1 head of broccoli,
cut into florets
1 small aubergine,
cut into cubes
400ml tin reduced-fat
coconut milk
200g basmati rice

For the curry paste

2 teaspoons ground coriander
1 teaspoon ground cumin
3 red chillies, deseeded and
finely chopped
1 lemongrass stalk,
roughly chopped
5cm piece ginger, peeled
and roughly chopped
Grated zest and juice
of 1 lime
2 shallots, finely chopped
3 garlic cloves,
roughly chopped
1 tablespoon fresh coriander,
chopped, plus extra to serve
1 tablespoon vegetable oil

1 Put all the curry paste ingredients in a mini food processor, and blitz to a rough purée. Add a little water to loosen the mixture. You could also make the paste in a pestle and mortar.

2 Mist a non-stick pan with the cooking spray and put over a medium heat. Add the curry paste and cook for 1-2 minutes or until fragrant.

3 Add the broccoli and aubergine, then cook for 6-8 minutes until the vegetables are just beginning to soften. Pour in the coconut milk and stir well to combine. Simmer for 10 minutes until the vegetables are tender and the sauce has thickened slightly.

4 Meanwhile, cook the rice according to the pack instructions, then drain well. Stir the extra coriander through the curry, then serve with the cooked rice.

Tip
Shop bought curry paste will work in this recipe too. Using 70g of paste will keep the SmartPoints the same.

10 SmartPoints value

SmartPoints
10 per serving

See page 6

Quorn fajitas with cheese & soured cream

Serves 4

Prep time
10 minutes

Cook time
15 minutes

Spicy Quorn pieces make a great substitute for chicken in these Mexican-style wraps.

Ingredients

Calorie controlled
cooking spray
2 x 350g packs Quorn pieces
1 red and 1 yellow pepper,
deseeded and sliced
1 red onion, sliced
2 teaspoons smoked paprika
2 teaspoons ground cumin
½ teaspoon chilli powder
4 Weight Watchers
White Wraps
4 tablespoons reduced-fat
soured cream
50g Weight Watchers
Reduced Fat Grated
Mature Cheese
Lime wedges, to serve

1 Preheat the oven to 200°C, fan 180°C, gas mark 6. Mist a wide frying pan with cooking spray, place over a medium heat and add the Quorn pieces. Cook for 5 minutes or until golden, then stir in the vegetables and spices, season to taste and cook for a further 8-10 minutes, or until the vegetables are just softened and lightly golden.

2 Meanwhile, cover the wraps with foil and heat in the oven for 8 minutes.

3 Top each wrap with a quarter of the fajita mixture, soured cream and cheese, then roll up and serve with the lime wedges.

SmartPoints
6 per serving

Soy-roasted aubergines with fragrant rice

Serves 4

Prep time
10 minutes
Cook time
40 minutes

Baby aubergines are marinated in Asian flavours, then oven-roasted until tender and succulent.

Ingredients
700g baby aubergines, halved lengthways
2 teaspoons sesame oil
1 tablespoon mirin
1 tablespoon agave nectar
2 tablespoons soy sauce
1 heaped teaspoon peanut butter
½ teaspoon chilli flakes
240g fragrant rice
150g frozen peas
Juice of 1 lime, plus wedges to serve
Small handful of fresh coriander, roughly chopped

1 Preheat the oven to 200°C, fan 180°C, gas mark 6. Put the aubergines in a large roasting tray. In a small bowl, whisk together the sesame oil, mirin, agave nectar, soy sauce, peanut butter and chilli flakes. Pour the marinade over the aubergines and stir well to ensure they are well covered. Roast in the oven for 35-40 minutes, or until tender and sticky.

2 Meanwhile, cook the rice according to pack instructions. Bring another pan of water to the boil and cook the peas for 3-4 minutes, then drain. Add the peas to the cooked rice, squeeze in the lime juice, season and stir through the fresh coriander, then serve with the roasted aubergines.

SmartPoints
9 per serving

See page 6

Tip
If you can't find baby aubergines, use larger ones. Cut them into quarters lengthwise, then cut each piece in half.

Lentil, apple & spinach salad with hazelnuts

Serves 4

Prep time
10 minutes

Cook time
25 minutes

This fresh-tasting salad makes a perfect dinner in the warmer months.

Ingredients

200g dried green lentils
1 litre vegetable stock, made with 1 stock cube
40g hazelnuts
1 celery stick, finely chopped
2 shallots, finely chopped
100g young leaf spinach
2 green apples
Juice of ½ lemon

For the dressing

2 tablespoons extra virgin olive oil
1 tablespoon red wine vinegar
1 teaspoon wholegrain mustard

1 Put the lentils in a saucepan and cover with the stock. Bring to the boil then simmer for 20-25 minutes, until tender but still with a little bite. Drain the lentils, then transfer to a large bowl

2 Meanwhile, toast the hazelnuts in a dry frying pan over a medium heat for 4-5 minutes until they are golden and fragrant, taking care not to let them burn. Roughly chop them (reserving a few whole ones to garnish), then mix them into the lentils, along with the celery, shallots and spinach.

3 Slice the apples into wedges and remove the core. Toss with the lemon juice to prevent them turning brown. Add to the salad.

4 Whisk together the dressing ingredients in a small bowl and season well. Pour over the salad and toss gently, then serve with the reserved hazelnuts sprinkled on top.

SmartPoints
5 per serving

See page 6

Tip

You could use 600g rinsed and drained tinned lentils instead of dried ones to speed this dish up.

White pizza with ricotta & asparagus

Serves 4

Prep time
15 minutes

Cook time
15 minutes

This easy pizza is topped with garlic-infused ricotta, instead of a traditional tomato sauce.

Ingredients
220g pizza dough (we used Northern Dough Co's rosemary frozen dough)
250g tub ricotta
2 garlic cloves, roughly chopped
250g asparagus, cut lengthways into thin strips
2 teaspoons capers
125g ball of light mozzarella, thinly sliced
Calorie controlled cooking spray

1 Preheat the oven to 220°C, fan 200°C, gas mark 7. Roll out the pizza dough into 2 x 30cm rounds and transfer to a non-stick pizza tray or flat baking sheet.

2 Put the ricotta in a mini food processor with the garlic cloves. Season and blitz until smooth and well combined.

3 Divide the ricotta mixture between the 2 pizza bases and spread evenly across the surface. Scatter over the asparagus and capers. Divide the mozzarella between the 2 pizzas, then mist each one with cooking spray. Bake in the oven for 12-15 minutes, or until the base is golden and crispy and the mozzarella has melted. Cut the pizzas in half and serve straight away.

SmartPoints
9 per serving

Baked sweet potatoes with veggie chilli

Serves 4

Prep time
10 minutes

Cook time
40 minutes

This tasty chilli can be used in all sorts of ways, like this topping for a jacket sweet potato.

Ingredients

4 sweet potatoes, about 150g each
Calorie controlled cooking spray
1 red onion, finely chopped
1 garlic clove, crushed
2 carrots, diced
1 red and 1 yellow pepper, deseeded and roughly chopped
1 teaspoon ground cumin
1 teaspoon chilli powder
½ teaspoon cayenne pepper
½ teaspoon cinnamon
2 x 400g tins chopped tomatoes
395g tin mixed beans in mild chilli sauce
150g frozen sweetcorn
½ medium avocado, sliced
4 tablespoons reduced-fat soured cream

1 Preheat the oven to 200°C, fan 180°C, gas mark 6. Put the sweet potatoes on a baking tray and bake for 35-40 minutes, or until tender.

2 Meanwhile, make the chilli. Mist a large pan with the cooking spray and cook the onion for 4-5 minutes until translucent. Add the garlic and cook for another minute.

3 Stir in the carrots and peppers, then sprinkle in all the spices. Stir well and cook for 1 minute. Season to taste.

4 Pour in the tomatoes and mixed beans, rinse out the tins with a splash of water and add that to the pan, then simmer for 18-20 minutes until the vegetables are cooked through. Add the sweetcorn and cook for a further 5 minutes.

5 To serve, slice open the sweet potatoes and spoon the chilli on top. Serve with the avocado slices and 1 tablespoon soured cream per person. You can freeze the chilli on its own.

SmartPoints
9 per serving

See page 6

Tofu kebabs & rice salad

Cubes of tofu are marinated with delicious Asian-style flavours, then griddled with fresh vegetables.

Serves 4

Prep time
15 minutes + pressing + marinating

Cook time
6-8 minutes

Ingredients
400g firm tofu
4 tablespoons soy sauce
Juice of 1 lime
3cm piece fresh ginger, peeled and grated
1 red chilli, finely sliced
Mixed vegetables, such as red pepper, aubergine and courgette, sliced or cubed
Calorie controlled cooking spray

For the rice salad
2 x 250g packs microwave brown rice, cooked to pack instructions
Bunch of spring onions, trimmed and sliced
Handful of fresh coriander, chopped
Juice of 1 lime, plus wedges to serve

You will also need
4 wooden skewers, soaked in cold water for 30 minutes to prevent burning

1 Wrap the tofu in kitchen paper and put on a plate. Put another plate on top and weigh it down using a full tin of food. Leave for 30 minutes to drain, then pour off the liquid and cut into 16 equal cubes.

2 Put the soy sauce, lime juice, ginger and chilli into a shallow bowl, mix well then add the tofu and stir gently until it's coated in the marinade. Cover and marinate in the fridge for 2 hours.

3 Thread the tofu onto the skewers, alternating with the veg. Mist with cooking spray. Cook for 3-4 minutes each side on a hot barbecue, or in a griddle pan over a medium-high heat, until the tofu is starting to caramelise and the vegetables are cooked.

4 Meanwhile, make the salad. Toss all the ingredients together in a serving bowl, then season well. Serve with the tofu kebabs and lime wedges.

Tip
Pressing the tofu first helps remove the excess water from it, so it can absorb all the flavours from the marinade.

SmartPoints
6 per serving

See page 6

Roasted mushroom pasta

Serves 4

Prep time
10 minutes

Cook time
35 minutes

Roasting mixed mushrooms gives this dish plenty of flavour, while the toasted breadcrumbs add crunch.

Ingredients
450g mixed mushrooms, cleaned and thickly sliced (we used chestnut, shiitake and portobello)
3 garlic cloves, bruised
1 sprig fresh rosemary, leaves picked
Zest of ½ lemon
100ml vegetable stock, made with ½ stock cube
1 tablespoon 0% fat natural Greek yogurt
3 slices Weight Watchers Sliced Brown Danish Bread
¼ teaspoon chilli flakes, crushed
¼ teaspoon sea salt flakes
¼ teaspoon freshly ground black pepper
Calorie controlled cooking spray
2 sprigs fresh thyme, leaves picked
400g wholewheat spaghetti
3 tablespoons fresh flat-leaf parsley, chopped, plus extra leaves to garnish

1 Preheat the oven to 200°C, fan 180°C, gas mark 6. Put the mushrooms, garlic, rosemary and lemon zest in a roasting tin. Pour over the stock, season well and cover with foil. Roast for 15 minutes. Remove the foil and roast for another 15 minutes. Let cool slightly, then stir in the yogurt.

2 Meanwhile, in a food processor, blitz the bread to fine crumbs then toss with the chilli, salt and pepper. Mist with cooking spray to coat.

3 Heat a frying pan over a medium heat. Add the crumbs and cook, stirring, for 2-3 minutes until crisp. Stir in the thyme, then cook for 1 minute, or until the breadcrumbs are golden.

4 Cook the spaghetti to pack instructions during the last 15 minutes of mushroom roasting time. Drain and toss with the mushrooms, their juices and the chopped parsley. Serve garnished with the toasted crumbs and parsley leaves.

SmartPoints
10 per serving

Roasted fennel, broad bean & ricotta salad

Serves 4

Prep time
15 minutes

Cook time
45 minutes

Fennel takes the starring role in this simple, warm salad that's topped with toasted breadcrumbs.

Ingredients
4 fennel bulbs, cut into wedges
1 tablespoon olive oil
50g white bread
200g broad beans (fresh or frozen)
250g tub ricotta
Zest and juice of 1 lemon, plus lemon wedges, to serve

1 Preheat the oven to 200°C, fan 180°C, gas mark 6. Put the fennel in a roasting tray and drizzle with oil. Season. Roast in the oven for 30-35 minutes, or until soft. Remove from the oven, transfer to a bowl and leave to cool. Set tray aside.

2 Blitz the bread to rough textured breadcrumbs in a mini food processor (or roughly chop with a knife). Place in the roasting tray you have used for the fennel and place in the oven. Cook for 6-8 minutes, or until crisp and golden. Remove from the oven, season and set aside.

3 Meanwhile, cook the broad beans in a pan of boiling water for around 4-5 minutes. Drain and refresh in a bowl of water to preserve their colour. Remove from their skins.

4 Mix the ricotta with the half the lemon zest and half the juice.

5 Toss the broad beans with the fennel and squeeze over the remaining lemon juice.

6 Divide the fennel salad between serving plates, sprinkle over the toasted breadcrumbs and serve with the lemon ricotta, garnished with the remaining lemon zest and lemon wedges.

Tip
You could save time by making the breadcrumbs in advance and storing in an airtight container for up to a week.

V **6 SmartPoints value**

SmartPoints
6 per serving

Pad Thai with satay sauce

Serves 4

Prep time
10 minutes
Cook time
5 minutes

A veggie version of the Thai restaurant favourite, this tasty dish is on the table in just 15 minutes.

Ingredients
Calorie controlled cooking spray
300g pack spiralised butternut squash
300g pack straight to wok ribbon rice noodles
4 spring onions, trimmed and finely sliced
100g young leaf spinach, roughly torn
Handful of fresh basil, leaves picked and torn
30g unsalted peanuts, chopped

For the sauce
2 tablespoons rice vinegar
2 tablespoons reduced-fat peanut butter
2 tablespoons light soy sauce
1 red chilli, finely chopped

1 Put a non-stick frying pan or wok over a medium heat and mist with the cooking spray. Add the butternut squash noodles and cook, stirring gently every now and then to avoid them breaking up, for 2-3 minutes until the noodles are cooked but still firm.

2 Add the rice noodles and cook, stirring gently, for a further 1-2 minutes until heated through.

3 Meanwhile, whisk together the sauce ingredients, along with 1 tablespoon water, until combined.

4 Remove the frying pan or wok from the heat and add the spring onions, spinach and basil, tossing everything together and letting the heat from the noodles wilt the spinach.

5 Divide the noodle mixture between plates and serve drizzled with the sauce and topped with the peanuts.

SmartPoints
7 per serving

See page 6

Quorn keema curry

Serves 4

Prep time
15 minutes

Cook time
35 minutes

Ingredients
Calorie controlled
cooking spray
1 onion, finely chopped
5cm piece fresh ginger,
peeled and grated
2 garlic cloves,
finely chopped
1 tablespoon garam masala
1 teaspoon ground cumin
1 teaspoon ground turmeric
200g potatoes, cut into
1.5cm cubes
400g tin chopped tomatoes
250g Quorn mince
150g frozen peas
240g brown rice
4 tablespoons 0% fat
natural Greek yogurt
Large handful of fresh
coriander, roughly chopped

A veggie version of a traditional, Indian-style curry that's made using Quorn mince, instead of meat.

1 Mist a large saucepan with the cooking spray and put over a medium heat. Add the onion and sauté for 5-6 minutes until its starts to soften and brown. Add the ginger and garlic, then cook for 1 minute, then add the spices and cook for a further minute.

2 Add the potatoes, chopped tomatoes and 200ml water. Bring to the boil, then reduce the heat, cover and simmer for 15 minutes. Remove the lid, add the Quorn and continue to cook, covered, for 10 minutes, adding the peas for the last 2 minutes.

3 Meanwhile, cook the rice to pack instructions. Drain and serve with the curry, a dollop of yogurt and the chopped coriander sprinkled over.

SmartPoints
7 per serving

See page 6

Black bean & avocado wraps

Avocado and black beans are wrapped in warm wholemeal tortillas with a zingy pineapple salsa.

Serves 4

Prep time
15 minutes

Cook time
10 minutes

Ingredients
Calorie controlled cooking spray
200g fresh pineapple, cut into chunks
100g cucumber, finely diced
½ red onion, finely chopped
1 red chilli, finely chopped
1 tablespoon lime juice
2 tablespoons fresh coriander, finely chopped
1 garlic clove, finely chopped
400g tin black beans, rinsed and drained
¼ teaspoon dried oregano
4 wholemeal wraps
60g baby spinach leaves
1 avocado, sliced

1 Spray a griddle pan with cooking spray and place over a medium-high heat. Add the pineapple and cook for 3 minutes on each side until beginning to char. Transfer to a plate and leave to cool, then roughly chop.

2 In a bowl, toss together the diced pineapple, cucumber, red onion, chilli, lime juice and coriander, seasoning well. Cover and put in the fridge.

3 Mist a frying pan with cooking spray and put over a medium heat. Add the garlic and cook for 1 minute. Add the beans, oregano and 150ml water. Cook over a medium heat, gently mashing the beans with the back of a wooden spoon, for 2-3 minutes until heated through and most of the liquid has evaporated. Remove from the heat, cover and set aside.

4 Meanwhile, heat the wraps according to pack instructions. Divide the spinach leaves and beans between the warmed wraps, then add a few slices of avocado and some pineapple salsa to each one. Fold in the top and bottom and roll up the wraps, then serve straight away.

SmartPoints
6 per serving

Jerk-style sweet potato curry

A Caribbean-inspired curry with loads of colourful veg, perfect served with cauliflower rice – see our tip.

Serves 4

Prep time
20 minutes

Cook time
45 minutes

Ingredients

Calorie controlled cooking spray
1 onion, finely chopped
3cm piece fresh ginger, peeled and roughly chopped
3 garlic cloves, roughly chopped
2 Scotch Bonnet chillies, halved and deseeded
1 tablespoon fresh rosemary, finely chopped
Small bunch of coriander, leaves and stalks separated
4 spring onions, trimmed and roughly chopped
½ tablespoon ground allspice
600g sweet potato, peeled and cut into 2-3cm pieces
400g tin kidney beans, drained and rinsed
2 red peppers, deseeded and roughly chopped
400ml tin light coconut milk
300ml vegetable stock, made with ½ stock cube
Lime wedges, to serve

1 Mist a large saucepan with cooking spray and put over a medium heat. Add the onion and cook for 8-10 minutes, until softened.

2 Meanwhile, put the ginger, garlic, chillies, rosemary, coriander stalks, spring onions and ground allspice in a mini food processor and blitz until you have a rough paste. Add to the onions and cook for 3 minutes, then add the sweet potato, kidney beans, red peppers, coconut milk and vegetable stock. Season to taste.

3 Bring to a simmer and cook, covered, for 20 minutes, or until the sweet potato is just cooked. Remove the lid and cook for a further 10 minutes, until the sauce has thickened slightly.

4 Stir the coriander leaves through the curry, then serve with lime wedges and cauliflower rice (see tip).

9 SmartPoints value

SmartPoints
9 per serving

See page 6

Tip
To make cauliflower rice, blitz 600g cauliflower in a food processor, then cook in a pan misted with cooking spray for 3-4 minutes.

Cajun-style tofu with corn salsa & crispy salad

Serves 4

Prep time
15 minutes + pressing

Cook time
25 minutes

Tofu is perfect for absorbing lots of other flavours – in this dish it's teamed with Cajun spices.

Ingredients
396g pack firm tofu
2 teaspoons dried thyme
1½ teaspoons sweet paprika
1 teaspoon smoked paprika
1 teaspoon dried oregano
½ teaspoon garlic granules
½ teaspoon cayenne pepper
Calorie controlled cooking spray
2 corn cobs
10 cherry tomatoes, halved
3 spring onions, finely sliced
1 red chilli, finely diced
Small handful of coriander, finely chopped
170g mixed salad leaves

1 Wrap the tofu in kitchen paper and put on a plate. Put another plate on top and weigh it down using a full tin of food. Leave for 30 minutes to drain, pour off the liquid and cut into 12 slices.

2 Combine the thyme, paprikas, oregano, garlic granules and cayenne pepper in a small bowl. Dust the tofu slices in the spices, then cover and set aside.

3 Mist a large griddle pan with cooking spray and put over a medium-high heat. Add the corn cobs and cook for 15-20 minutes, turning occasionally until they are evenly charred.

4 Remove from the heat and let cool slightly. Use a sharp knife to slice the corn kernels off the cobs. Leave to cool completely then toss with the cherry tomatoes, spring onions, chilli and coriander. Set aside.

5 Reheat the griddle pan and mist again with cooking spray. Add the tofu and cook on both sides for 3 minutes. Arrange the salad leaves on plates and top with the corn salsa and tofu.

SmartPoints
0 per serving

See page 6

Pulled celeriac burgers with apple slaw

Serves 4

Prep time
15 minutes

Cook time
2 hours 40 minutes

Yes – pulled celeriac! Trust us, it has a wonderful, smoky flavour, and a great texture.

Ingredients
1 celeriac, peeled and halved
Calorie controlled cooking spray
4 x 60g burger buns

For the sauce
400g passata
2 tablespoons honey
3 tablespoons dark soy sauce
1 tablespoon molasses
2 tablespoons cider vinegar
1 tablespoon tomato purée
2 teaspoons smoked paprika
1 teaspoon dried oregano
1 teaspoon cayenne pepper
2 garlic cloves, chopped
½ teaspoon ground cumin
1 teaspoon Tabasco

For the apple slaw
100g red cabbage, shredded
1 small Granny Smith apple, cored and cut into matchsticks
3 spring onions, sliced
50g half-fat crème fraîche
1 tablespoon cider vinegar
1 tablespoon flat-leaf parsley, finely chopped

1 Preheat the oven to 180°C, fan 160°C, gas mark 4. Put the celeriac on a baking tray and mist with the cooking spray. Rub all over, then cover in foil. Bake for 20 minutes.

2 Meanwhile, make the sauce by mixing all the sauce ingredients together in a small jug. Remove the celeriac from the oven and pour over half the sauce. Cover with the foil and return to the oven for 1 hour.

3 Remove from the oven and gently pull apart with two forks. Ladle over a little more of the sauce and cover again. Bake for a further 40 minutes. Remove from the oven, pull again, ladle over the remaining sauce and bake for a final 40 minutes. Pull again and gently stir together, scrapping in the dark sticky edges. Leave to cool slightly before serving.

4 Put all the slaw ingredients in a bowl, season to taste and toss everything together. Layer the coleslaw and celeriac between the burger buns, then serve.

SmartPoints
9 per serving

80

Serves 4

Prep time
15 minutes

Cook time
55 minutes

Goat's cheese, sage & butternut squash pies

A winning combination of crisp pastry, tangy goat's cheese and sweet butternut squash.

Ingredients

1 small or ½ large butternut squash, peeled, deseeded and cut into 2cm cubes

Calorie controlled cooking spray

4 sheets of filo pastry

125g soft goat's cheese, chopped

6 sage leaves, chopped

Mixed salad leaves, to serve

1 Preheat the oven to 200°C, fan 180°C, gas mark 6. Spread the butternut squash out over a large baking sheet, mist with cooking spray and season. Roast for 20 minutes, then turn and roast for a further 20-25 minutes, until soft and golden. Remove from the oven and set aside to cool slightly.

2 Meanwhile, cut each sheet of filo pastry widthways into 3 equal pieces and use to line the holes of a deep 12-hole muffin tray. Fill with the cooled roasted butternut squash, goat's cheese and sage, then bring up the sides of the filo pastry and scrunch together at the top to create parcels. Mist with cooking spray and bake for 10 minutes, until golden.

3 Serve 3 pies per person, with the green salad on the side.

SmartPoints
7 per serving

Moroccan-style veggie shepherd's pie

We've pepped up our lentil shepherd's pie with aromatic Moroccan spices.

Serves 4

Prep time
20 minutes + resting

Cook time
1 hour 25 minutes

Ingredients
1 large butternut squash, halved and deseeded (about 1kg prepared weight)
Calorie controlled cooking spray
1 onion, finely chopped
2 large carrots, finely diced
2 celery sticks, finely chopped
250g chestnut mushrooms, sliced
2 garlic cloves, crushed
1 teaspoon ground cumin
1 teaspoon ground cinnamon
¼ teaspoon chilli flakes
400g tin green lentils in water
400g tin chopped tomatoes
250ml vegetable stock, made with ½ stock cube
Handful fresh flat-leaf parsley, roughly chopped

1 Preheat the oven to 200°C, fan 180°C, gas mark 6. Mist the butternut squash with cooking spray and put on a baking tray, cut-side up. Season and roast for 1 hour or until tender. Set aside to cool slightly and reduce the oven temperature to 180°C, fan 160°C, gas mark 4. Once cool, scoop out the roasted flesh and mash until smooth, seasoning well.

2 While the squash is roasting, mist a large non-stick frying pan with cooking spray and cook the onion, carrots and celery over a medium heat for 8-10 minutes, until softened. Add the mushrooms, garlic and spices, then cook for a further 2 minutes. Stir in the lentils (including the water from the tin), chopped tomatoes and stock. Season, bring to the boil then simmer, covered, for 10 minutes.

3 Transfer the lentil mixture to a 20cm square pie dish. Spoon over the mash, making sure that none of the lentil mixture is visible. Cook for 25 minutes until piping hot. Let rest for 10 minutes then serve garnished with the parsley.

SmartPoints
0 per serving

See page 6

Tip
You can reduce the cooking time for the squash to 30 minutes by peeling and cutting it into cubes.

Cauliflower shawarma in toasted wraps

Serves 4

Prep time
10 minutes

Cook time
45 minutes

Tossing cauliflower and chickpeas in spices before roasting gives them a delicious texture and flavour.

Ingredients

1 large cauliflower, broken into florets
400g tin chickpeas, drained and rinsed
1 teaspoon sweet paprika
1 teaspoon cumin
1 teaspoon turmeric
½ teaspoon cinnamon
½ teaspoon chilli flakes
Juice of 2 lemons
1 tablespoon olive oil
4 large vine tomatoes, finely diced
1 red onion, finely sliced
125g 0% fat natural Greek yogurt
Small handful mint leaves, roughly chopped
4 Weight Watchers White Wraps

1 Preheat the oven to 200°C, fan 180°C, gas mark 6. Put the cauliflower and chickpeas into a large roasting tray. Mix all of the spices together and sprinkle over the cauliflower and chickpeas. Drizzle over half the lemon juice and the oil, then season to taste. Stir to ensure that the cauliflower and chickpeas are coated. Roast for 40-45 minutes, or until the cauliflower is golden and tender.

2 Meanwhile, in a bowl, mix together the tomatoes, onion and remaining lemon juice. Season to taste and set aside. In a small jug, mix together the yogurt and chopped mint. Season to taste.

3 When the cauliflower is roasted, remove from the oven and set aside. Cover the wraps in kitchen foil and put in the oven to heat for 8 minutes. Serve them filled with the cauliflower and chickpeas, topped with the tomato salad and a drizzle of yogurt.

SmartPoints
5 per serving

Asian-style grain bowl

This dish is inspired by Asian cuisine, but we've thrown in some Brussels sprouts for good measure!

Serves 4

Prep time
15 minutes

Cook time
40 minutes

Ingredients

Calorie controlled
cooking spray
½ red cabbage, finely sliced
2 garlic cloves, crushed
1 tablespoon grated ginger
1 tablespoon soy sauce
2 tablespoons rice vinegar
2 star anise
300g sweet potatoes, peeled
and cut into 2cm pieces
500g Brussels sprouts
200g brown rice
4 eggs
3 spring onions, finely sliced

1 Heat the oven to 200°C, fan 180°C, gas mark 6. Mist a pan with cooking spray and set over a medium heat. Add the red cabbage and cook for 10 minutes with the lid on.

2 Reduce the heat to medium-low. Add the garlic, ginger, soy sauce, rice vinegar and star anise to the pan. Pour in a generous splash of water, cover and cook for a further 30 minutes, until the cabbage is just cooked, stirring regularly.

3 Meanwhile, spread out the sweet potato pieces in a roasting tin, then mist with cooking spray and season to taste. Cook in the oven for 35 minutes, turning halfway through. Put the sprouts in another roasting tin and add to the oven for the last 20 minutes, until just cooked through.

4 Cook the rice to pack instructions.

5 Put a non-stick frying pan over a medium heat, mist with cooking spray and crack the eggs into the pan. Cook for 4-5 minutes, or until done to your liking.

6 Divide the rice between 4 bowls then top with red cabbage, sweet potatoes and Brussels sprouts. Top each bowl with a fried egg, then scatter over the spring onions to serve.

SmartPoints
8 per serving

See page 6

Quorn moussaka

Serves 4

Prep time
20 minutes
Cook time
55 minutes

For a healthy, vegetarian twist, we've used Quorn in place of the usual lamb in this Greek favourite.

Ingredients

Calorie controlled
cooking spray
2 large onions, halved
and sliced
3 garlic cloves, chopped
400g tin chopped tomatoes
2 tablespoons tomato purée
400ml vegetable stock,
made with 1 cube
½ teaspoon ground
cinnamon
3 bay leaves
½ teaspoon dried oregano
200g potatoes, peeled,
halved and sliced
1 large aubergine, trimmed
halved and sliced
350g pack Quorn mince
250g fat-free fromage frais
1 egg
25g light feta, crumbled
Finely chopped parsley,
to garnish

1 Preheat the oven to 180°C, fan 160°C, gas mark 4. Meanwhile, heat a lidded flameproof and ovenproof dish, over a medium heat, mist with the cooking spray then add the onions and garlic. Stir well, then cover and cook for just under 10 minutes, stirring occasionally. Add a splash of water if they start to stick.

2 Add the tinned tomatoes, purée and stock to the dish, then stir in the cinnamon, bay leaves and oregano. Stir well, then add the potato and aubergine slices.

3 Cover and leave to simmer for 20 minutes, or until the aubergine is soft and the potatoes are tender. Remove from the heat and stir in the Quorn.

4 Beat the fromage frais with the egg and feta cheese, then spread over the Quorn mixture and season to taste. Bake in the oven for 25 minutes until the topping is set, then scatter over the chopped parsley and serve.

SmartPoints
3 per serving

See page 6

Roasted vegetable quiche

It might look like pastry, but we've used potato to make the crust for this delicious quiche.

Serves 6

Prep time
25 minutes + cooling

Cook time
1 hour 30 minutes

Ingredients
750g Maris Piper potatoes, peeled and grated
½ teaspoon salt
Calorie controlled cooking spray
2 egg yolks
1 red pepper, deseeded and sliced
1 red onion, cut into thin wedges
1 courgette, cut into 1cm rounds
150g half-fat crème fraîche
150ml semi-skimmed milk
3 whole eggs
50g light feta cheese, crumbled
Large handful fresh basil, roughly chopped
Salad leaves, to serve

1 Preheat the oven to 200°C, fan 180°C, gas mark 6. Put the grated potatoes in a sieve set over a bowl and sprinkle with salt. Leave for 10 minutes until the excess moisture has drained out. Meanwhile, mist the sides of a 20cm springform cake tin with cooking spray, and line the bottom with baking paper.

2 Tip the potatoes onto a clean tea towel and squeeze out any further moisture. Put in a bowl and stir in the egg yolks, then transfer the mixture to the lined cake tin. Using your fingers, spread the mixture over the base and about 5cm up the sides of the tin. Bake in the oven for 35-40 minutes or until golden brown, then set aside to cool.

3 At the same time as the crust is cooking, put the pepper, onion and courgette on a roasting tray and cook for 30-35 minutes, turning over halfway through, until golden brown and softened. Remove from the oven and set aside to cool. Reduce the oven temperature to 160°C, fan 140°C, gas mark 3.

4 Lightly whisk the crème fraîche, milk and whole eggs together in a bowl, then stir in the cooled roasted vegetables, feta and basil. Season to taste. Pour the mixture into the cooled potato crust and return to the oven for 45-50 minutes, until just set. Leave to cool for 15 minutes before removing from the tin. Serve warm with the salad leaves.

SmartPoints
6 per serving

See page 6

Cheesy pasta bake with butternut squash & sage

Puréed squash creates a velvety smooth sauce in this delicious mac'n'cheese-style dish.

Serves 4

Prep time
15 minutes

Cook time
40 minutes

Ingredients

1 butternut squash, peeled and cubed
150ml vegetable stock, made with ½ cube
1 teaspoon smoked paprika
Pinch grated nutmeg
1 onion, finely chopped
2 garlic cloves, crushed
2 tablespoons fresh sage leaves, chopped, plus a few whole leaves to serve
400g fusilli pasta
25g fresh breadcrumbs
25g Weight Watchers Mature Reduced-fat grated cheese

1 Preheat the oven to 200°C, fan 180°C, gas mark 6. Bring a large pan of water to the boil and add the butternut squash. Cook for 12-15 minutes until tender, then drain well.

2 Transfer the cooked squash to a blender and add the stock, paprika, nutmeg, chopped onion and garlic. Season to taste and blend until smooth. Stir the chopped sage leaves into the butternut squash sauce. Set aside.

3 Meanwhile, bring another large pan of water to the boil and cook the pasta for a couple of minutes less than the recommended cooking time. Drain well, reserving a cup of the cooking water.

4 Put the pasta back into the pan and pour in the sauce. Stir to combine, adding a little of the reserved cooking water. Transfer to a large baking dish.

5 Mix the breadcrumbs with the grated cheese and fresh whole sage leaves. Sprinkle on top, then put the dish into the oven and bake for 20-25 minutes until golden and bubbling.

SmartPoints
10 per serving

Beetroot & bean burgers with veggie chips

Serves 4

Prep time
30 minutes

Cook time
45 minutes

Burger and chips is a great weekend treat. Our version is much healthier and more colourful.

Ingredients
Calorie controlled cooking spray
1 red onion, finely diced
350g carrots, cut into chips
350g parsnips, peeled and cut into chips
350g butternut squash, peeled and cut into chips
400g raw beetroot, peeled and quartered
400g tin black beans, drained and rinsed
2 eggs, beaten
50g fresh white breadcrumbs
1 teaspoon smoked paprika
1 teaspoon ground cumin
100g 0% fat natural Greek yogurt
1 teaspoon ras el hanout
4 brioche-style burger buns, split, to serve
Lettuce leaves, to serve

1 Preheat the oven to 200°C, fan 180°C, gas mark 6. Meanwhile, mist a small pan with cooking spray, put over a medium heat and add the onion. Cook for 8-10 minutes, until just softened, then set aside to cool.

2 Spread the carrot, parsnip and butternut squash chips onto a large tray and mist with cooking spray. Season to taste and roast for 45 minutes, turning halfway through, until golden brown all over and cooked through.

3 Put the beetroot in a food processor and blitz until broken into small pieces, then add the black beans and pulse again to a rough purée. Transfer the mixture to a bowl and add the onion, beaten egg, breadcrumbs, paprika and cumin. Season to taste and mix well, then form the mixture into 4 patties.

4 Mist a non-stick pan with cooking spray and cook the burgers for 4-5 minutes on each side, then transfer to a roasting tray and cook in the oven for the final 20 minutes of the vegetable roasting time.

5 Mix the Greek yogurt with the ras el hanout. Serve the burgers in the buns with the lettuce leaves, a spoonful of the yogurt, and the vegetable chips on the side. You can freeze the burgers on their own.

SmartPoints
11 per serving

Tip
If you serve this with salad, instead of the buns, the SmartPoints will be just 6 per serving.

Creamy vegetable bake

Serves 4

Prep time
20 minutes
Cook time
1 hour 20 minutes

This colourful creamy, cheesy dish is everything you could want for on a chilly evening.

Ingredients
Calorie controlled
cooking spray
100ml vegetable stock,
made with ½ cube
300ml half-fat crème fraîche
2 garlic cloves, crushed
½ butternut squash, peeled
and sliced into thin rounds
1 large courgette, trimmed
and thinly sliced
1 large potato, peeled and
thinly sliced
1 fennel bulb, sliced
1 onion, sliced
1 tablespoon fresh
thyme leaves
30g Weight Watchers Mature
Reduced-fat grated cheese

1 Preheat the oven to 200°C, fan 180°C, gas mark 6.

2 Mist a large baking dish with the cooking spray. Combine the stock, crème fraîche and garlic in a jug and season to taste.

3 Layer the sliced vegetables in the dish, sprinkling thyme on top of each layer as you go. Pour over the crème fraîche and stock mixture.

4 Cover the dish tightly with foil and bake for 1 hour. Remove the foil, sprinkle over the cheese and bake for another 15-20 minutes, until the dish is golden and bubbling.

SmartPoints
7 per serving

See page 6

Ribollita

Serves 4

Prep time
15 minutes
Cook time
46 minutes

A classic, hearty soup originally from Tuscany, made with veggies, beans and leftover bread.

Ingredients

1 tablespoon olive oil
1 large onion, finely chopped
1 large carrot, finely diced
2 celery sticks, finely diced
3 garlic cloves, crushed
1 teaspoon fennel seeds
1 teaspoon mixed
dried herbs
400g tin chopped tomatoes
400g tin cannellini beans,
rinsed and drained
120g pack cavolo nero (black
kale), shredded, with any
thick stems removed
150g rustic white bread,
torn into chunks
4 eggs
1 tablespoon vegetarian
Italian hard cheese, shaved

1 Heat the olive oil in a pan. Add the onion, carrot and celery, then cook slowly for 8-10 minutes or until soft. Season to taste, then stir in the garlic, fennel seeds and dried herbs. Cook for another minute.

2 Pour in the chopped tomatoes and beans, along with a good splash of water. Simmer for 5 minutes, then add the cavolo nero and chunks of bread. Cover and cook on a low heat for another 30 minutes, checking occasionally if it needs more water.

3 Just before serving, poach the eggs in a pan of simmering water for 2-3 minutes. Spoon the soup into 4 bowls and serve with a poached egg on top, then scatter over the cheese and freshly ground black pepper. You can freeze the soup on its own.

SmartPoints
5 per serving

Tip
When poaching the eggs, create a gentle whirlpool in the water to help the egg white wrap around the yolk.

Spicy bean & squash stew

Serves 4

Prep time
15 minutes

Cook time
40 minutes

This is the perfect comfort food for a chilly day – beans and roasted squash with warming spices.

Ingredients

1 large butternut squash, peeled and cut into 2cm cubes
1 tablespoon vegetable oil
Handful fresh parsley, roughly chopped
Calorie controlled cooking spray
1 red onion, finely chopped
2 garlic cloves, finely sliced
1 romano red pepper, deseeded and finely sliced
1 teaspoon cumin
2 teaspoons smoked paprika
½ teaspoon cinnamon
2 x 400g tins chopped tomatoes
400g tin butter beans, drained and rinsed
1 tablespoon red wine vinegar
2 teaspoons agave syrup
160g giant couscous
75g 0% fat natural Greek yogurt

1 Preheat the oven to 200°C, fan 180°C, gas mark 6. Put the squash in a large roasting tin and drizzle over the oil. Season well. Roast in the oven for 35-40 minutes, or until soft, then remove from the oven and stir through half the chopped parsley.

2 Meanwhile, mist a large pan with cooking spray and put over a medium heat. Fry the onion for 4-5 minutes, or until soft. Add the garlic and cook for a further 1 minute, then add the pepper. Cook for 5-6 minutes, or until softened, then add the spices and cook for a further 1 minute.

3 Add the tomatoes, butter beans, vinegar and agave syrup, then stir well to combine. Simmer gently for around 20 minutes, or until the liquid has reduced.

4 Meanwhile, prepare the couscous to pack instructions and stir through the remaining chopped parsley.

5 Serve the stew with the couscous, topped with the roasted squash and a dollop of yogurt.

SmartPoints
6 per serving

Tofu pho

Pronounced 'fuh', this is a traditional Vietnamese dish. We've used marinated tofu instead of meat.

Serves 4

Prep time
10 minutes + pressing + marinating

Cook time
45 minutes

Ingredients
396g pack firm tofu
2 tablespoons hoisin sauce
3 tablespoons dark soy sauce
1 tablespoon rice wine vinegar
Calorie controlled cooking spray
3 garlic cloves, sliced
5cm piece root ginger, peeled and thickly sliced
1 onion, cut into wedges
1.5 litres vegetable stock, made with 3 stock cubes
1 tablespoon miso paste
100g thick rice noodles
2 pak choi bulbs, trimmed and halved
1 courgette, trimmed and spiralised
1 teaspoon sesame seeds

1 Wrap the tofu in kitchen paper and put on a plate. Put another plate on top and weigh it down using a full tin of food. Leave for 30 minutes to drain, pour off the liquid and cut into 12 slices.

2 Combine the hoisin, 1 tablespoon of the soy sauce and the vinegar in a small bowl. Put the tofu slices in a shallow dish and pour over the marinade. Leave to marinate for 20 minutes.

3 Mist a large pan with cooking spray and put over a medium-high heat. Add the garlic, ginger and onion, then cook for 6-8 minutes, stirring occasionally, until golden.

4 Add 2 ladles of the stock and stir to deglaze the pan. Add the rest of the stock and the remaining soy sauce. Bring to a simmer over a medium heat, then reduce the heat to low and cover. Simmer for 30 minutes, then strain and return the broth to the pan with the miso paste.

5 Meanwhile, cook the tofu. Mist a large griddle pan with cooking spray and put over a medium-high heat. Add the tofu and cook on each side for 3 minutes until griddle marks show.

6 Meanwhile, soak the noodles in boiling water for 4 minutes, then drain, cover with cold water and set aside. Add the pak choi to the broth and cook for 3 minutes until just wilted. Stir in the courgetti, and cook for a further 1 minute.

7 Divide the noodles between 4 serving bowls, then ladle over the broth and vegetables. Top with the tofu and sprinkle over the sesame seeds, then serve.

SmartPoints
5 per serving

Mushroom & chestnut pie

Serves 4

Prep time
15 minutes + cooling
Cook time
50 minutes

Unlike other nuts, chestnuts are low in fat and calories, and they go perfectly with mushrooms.

Ingredients
15g butter
1 onion, finely chopped
2 garlic cloves, finely sliced
10g dried wild mushrooms, soaked in hot water
650g mixed mushrooms, roughly chopped
140g vacuum-packed chestnuts, roughly chopped
1 tablespoon fresh thyme leaves
30g plain flour
250ml semi-skimmed milk
3 sheets filo pastry
Calorie controlled cooking spray
2 tablespoons vegetarian Italian hard cheese, grated

1 Preheat the oven to 200°C, fan 180°C, gas mark 6. Melt the butter in a large pan over a medium heat. Fry the onion for 3-4 minutes, or until soft. Add the garlic and cook for 2 minutes.

2 Drain the soaked dried mushrooms and reserve the soaking liquid. Then add all of the mushrooms to the pan and cook for 5-6 minutes, stirring frequently, until the mushrooms are soft. Add a splash of the soaking water to help the mushrooms cook down, and to add flavour.

3 Add the chestnuts and thyme, then sprinkle over the flour. Cook for 2 minutes, then slowly add the milk, a little at a time, stirring well after each addition to avoid any lumps.

4 When all the milk has been added, continue to cook, stirring frequently until the sauce thickens, then set aside to cool.

5 Transfer the cooled mushroom mixture to a pie dish. Mist each sheet of filo with calorie controlled spray and roughly crumple up. Put on top of the pie so the filling is completely covered. Scatter over the cheese. Bake for 20-25 minutes, or until the pastry is golden, then serve.

SmartPoints
9 per serving

Turmeric broth bowl with beans, veg & noodles

Serves 4

Prep time
15 minutes

Cook time
40 minutes

The turmeric gives the dish an appealing, sunshine-like colour, while the ginger adds a gentle heat.

Ingredients

1 small butternut squash, peeled and cut into 2cm cubes
1 large fennel bulb, thickly sliced
Calorie controlled cooking spray
1 tablespoon turmeric
2 garlic cloves, crushed
10cm piece fresh ginger, peeled and grated
2 nests wholewheat noodles
410g tin cannellini beans, drained and rinsed
Small handful fresh coriander, chopped
Lime wedges, to serve

1 Preheat the oven to 200°C, 180°C, gas mark 6. Put the butternut squash and fennel into a roasting tin and mist with the cooking spray, then season well. Roast for 30 minutes until tender and golden brown.

2 Meanwhile, put 1.5 litres water into a large pan along with the turmeric, garlic and ginger. Bring to the boil, season then simmer on a low heat until the veggies have finished roasting.

3 Add the noodles, drained beans and roasted vegetables to the soup. Simmer for 8-10 minutes until the noodles are cooked through, then divide between 4 bowls.

4 Serve sprinkled with the fresh coriander and a lime wedge to squeeze over.

SmartPoints
3 per serving

Tip
If you have fresh turmeric instead of the powdered version, then use a thumb-sized piece, peeled and grated.

Roasted cauliflower with spicy lentils

Roasting cauliflower gives it a completely different texture and a lovely caramelised taste.

Serves 4

Prep time
10 minutes

Cook time
1 hour 30 minutes

Ingredients
1 large cauliflower
125g 0% fat natural Greek yogurt
1 tablespoon harissa paste
Calorie controlled cooking spray
1 red onion, finely chopped
1 carrot, finely chopped
2 garlic cloves, finely chopped
1 teaspoon cumin
1 teaspoon coriander
½ teaspoon chilli flakes
400g tin chopped tomatoes
240g dried green lentils
1 litre vegetable stock, made with 1 stock pot
150g young leaf spinach
75g light feta cheese

1 Preheat the oven to 200°C, fan 180°C, gas mark 6. Remove the outer leaves from the cauliflower and slice the bottom so it sits flat, then put it in a small roasting dish.

2 Mix together the yogurt and harissa, then spread it over the cauliflower. Cover the roasting dish with a large sheet of foil and put in the oven to roast for 1½ hours, removing the foil for the final 30 minutes.

3 Meanwhile, mist a large non-stick frying pan with cooking spray. Fry the onion and carrot for 5-6 minutes, or until they start to soften. Add the garlic and continue to cook for a further 2 minutes. Stir in the spices and cook for a further 1 minute. Add the tomatoes, lentils and stock and bring to the boil. Reduce to a simmer. Simmer for 20 minutes, or until the liquid has reduced and the lentils are cooked. Turn off the heat and add the spinach. Cover and wait for the spinach to wilt, then give it a stir and season to taste.

4 Crumble the feta cheese over the lentils, then serve with the roasted cauliflower.

SmartPoints
1 per serving

See page 6

Recipe index

SmartPoints index

weight watchers
SmartP●ints®